T0071144

Cecilia McDowall

A Time for all Seasons
Before Words Fail

for soprano solo, upper voices, SSATB, piano, and optional percussion

MUSIC DEPARTMENT

OXFORD
UNIVERSITY PRESS

OXFORD
UNIVERSITY PRESS

Great Clarendon Street, Oxford, OX2 6DP,
United Kingdom

Oxford University Press is a department of the University of Oxford.
It furthers the University's objective of excellence in research, scholarship,
and education by publishing worldwide. Oxford is a registered trade mark of
Oxford University Press in the UK and in certain other countries

© Oxford University Press 2016

Cecilia McDowall has asserted her right under the Copyright, Designs
and Patents Act, 1988, to be identified as the Composer of this Work

First published in 2016

Impression: 1

All rights reserved. No part of this publication may be reproduced,
stored in a retrieval system, or transmitted, in any form or by any means,
without the prior permission in writing of Oxford University Press

Permission to perform this work in public
(except in the course of divine worship) should normally be obtained from
a local performing right licensing organization, unless the owner or the occupier
of the premises being used already holds a licence from such an organization.
Likewise, permission to make and exploit a recording of this work
should be obtained from a local mechanical copyright licensing organization

Enquiries concerning reproduction outside the scope of the above
should be directed to the Music Rights Department, Oxford University Press,
at music.permissions.uk@oup.com or at the address above

ISBN 978–0–19–341148–7

Printed in Great Britain on acid-free paper by
Halstan & Co. Ltd, Amersham, Bucks

Composer's note

At the heart of *A Time for all Seasons* lies the extraordinary text from Ecclesiastes 3: 1–8—'To every thing there is a season'. The poetry of these universal and familiar words has been set in context by the award-winning author and poet Kevin Crossley-Holland, who, by reworking these verses, has brought a present-day perspective to the cantata in a subtle and evocative fashion.

The upper (or children's) voices thread a running commentary in both the first and last sections; at the start they sing an abbreviated first line of the Ecclesiastes text, and in the last—'There is nothing new under the sun'—present a prescient reminder of how things are and will be. The choir begins the work in a joyous mood, but then moves on to a more contemplative appraisal of reality. The soprano solo brings a relaxed and slightly jazzy flavour to the words 'When sudden birdsong is alarming', but is cut off by the return of the opening choral material.

In the bright middle section the upper voices sing the words of Ecclesiastes—'a time to plant, and a time to pluck up that which is planted'—with interjections from the sopranos and altos of the main choir. The soprano solo leads into the final section which, in the face of possible catastrophe, urges us to draw 'near to your creator'. Underlying the closing part of the work is a phrase taken from the 13th-century Latin sequence *Dies irae*—a musical premonition, perhaps, of things to come. The upper voices have the last word.

The work was originally conceived for soprano solo, children's choir, community choir, SSATB chorus, piano, and optional percussion. Here, the children's choir and community choir parts have been combined into a single part for upper voices, which could be performed equally well by an upper-voice, children's, or community choir.

Separate parts for upper-voice choir and percussion are available to download from www.oup.com.

A Time for all Seasons was commissioned by Harlow Chorus for its 40th anniversary. It was first performed in April 2016 by Emily Yarrow (soprano), Susan Graham Smith (piano), Graham Instrall (percussion), Harlow Chorus, Harlow Chorus Training Choir, and Harlow Children's Choir, conducted by Alexander Chaplin.

Duration: *c.*18 minutes

Text

A Time for all Seasons
Before Words Fail

To every thing there is a season, and a time to every purpose under the heaven:
A time to be born, and a time to die;

Before shoulders sag and stick-legs buckle,
before teeth rattle and eyes grow misty

Before heights become fearsome and
journeys troublesome

When sudden birdsong is alarming, and
sweet daughters sing out of tune

When even honey bees are irksome though
the apple is in blossom

Before desire slackens

Before the alphabet scrambles, before
words fail:

a time to plant, and a time to pluck up that which is planted;
A time to kill, and a time to heal; a time to break down, and a time to build up;
A time to weep, and a time to laugh; a time to mourn, and a time to dance;
A time to cast away stones, and a time to gather stones together; a time to embrace, and a time to refrain from embracing;
A time to get, and a time to lose; a time to keep, and a time to cast away;
A time to rend, and a time to sew; a time to keep silence, and a time to speak;
A time to love, and a time to hate; a time of war, and a time of peace.

The wind drives south, the wind
wafts north...
One generation stumbles, the next skips
and dances in...
There is nothing new under the sun

Before deadly clouds mass and close ranks

Before grids seize and turbines fall silent,
before the sea curdles

Before plates grind and widen and this poor
planet spins

Before the hub blackens and explodes,
before the moon wastes and constellations
are snuffed out

Before dust falls to dust and the spirit soars:
with a handful of quietness draw near to
your creator.

Ecclesiastes 3: 1–8 (King James Version)
Kevin Crossley-Holland (b. 1941)

Commissioned by Harlow Chorus in their 40th anniversary season

A Time for all Seasons

Before Words Fail

Kevin Crossley-Holland (b. 1941)
Ecclesiastes 3, vv.1–8

CECILIA McDOWALL

*Optional Percussion: Suspended Cymbal, Tambourine, Triangle

Music © Oxford University Press 2016. Text © Kevin Crossley-Holland 2016.

Printed in Great Britain

OXFORD UNIVERSITY PRESS, MUSIC DEPARTMENT, GREAT CLARENDON STREET, OXFORD OX2 6DP

The Moral Rights of the Composer have been asserted. Photocopying this copyright material is ILLEGAL

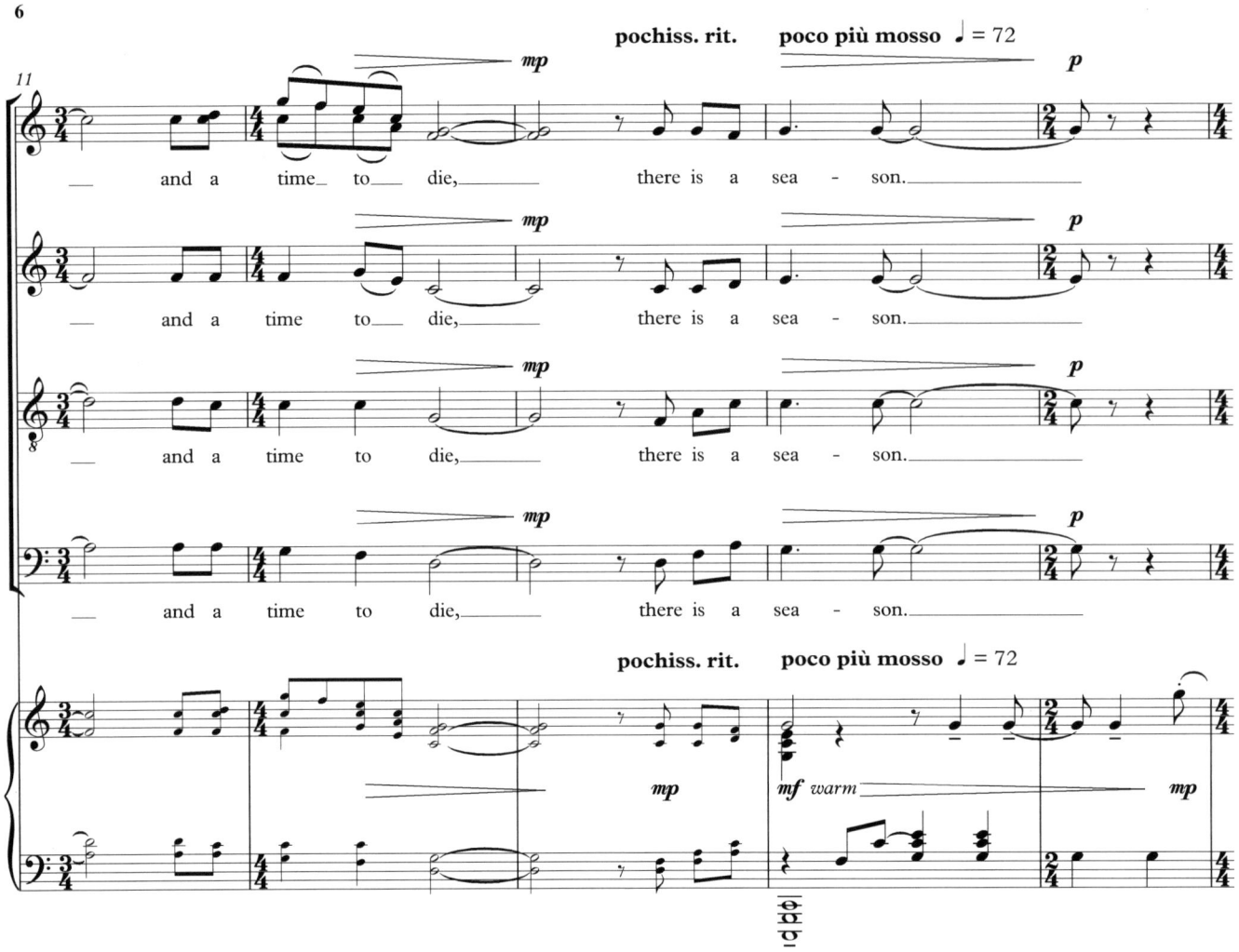
11
pochiss. rit.
poco più mosso ♩ = 72
mp
p
and a time to die, there is a sea - son.
and a time to die, there is a sea - son.
and a time to die, there is a sea - son.
and a time to die, there is a sea - son.
pochiss. rit.
poco più mosso ♩ = 72
mp
mf warm
mp

16
A
mf
Be -
mf
Be -
A
dolce e molto cantabile
mf

* This part may alternatively be sung by a children's choir

27
mf
To ev - 'ry thing a sea - son,
sag,
sag,
mf
and stick legs buck-le,
mf
and stick legs buck-le,
mf
To ev - 'ry thing a sea - son,
mp
mf
B
31
f
be - fore teeth rat-tle, rat - tle, and eyes grow
f
be - fore teeth rat-tle, rat - tle, and eyes grow
f
be - fore teeth rat-tle, rat - tle, and eyes grow
f
be - fore teeth rat-tle, rat - tle, and eyes grow
B
f

36
Sus Cym. (soft sticks)
Cym.
U.V.
To ev-'rything a sea - son,
S.
mist - y,
Be - fore
A.
mist - y,
Be - fore
T.
mist - y,
B.
mist - y,
40
heights, heights, be - come fear - some
heights, heights be - come, be - come fear - some
and jour - neys,
and jour -

45
mf
To ev - 'ry thing a sea - son,
and jour - neys, jour - neys trou-ble-some.
To ev - 'ry thing a sea - son
-neys, and jour - neys, jour-neys trou - ble - some.
To ev - 'ry thing a sea - son
mf
f

49
C
mf
Be - fore shoul-ders sag
Be - fore shoul-ders sag
sag
sag
C

53
Sus Cym. (soft sticks)
mf
f
To ev - 'ry thing a sea - son,
and stick legs buck - le,
Be - fore heights,
and stick legs buck - le,
Be - fore heights,
and stick legs buck-le,
Be - fore heights,
and stick legs buck-le,
Be-fore heights,
57
heights, heights, heights, heights, heights be - come
heights, heights, heights, heights, heights be - come
heights, heights, heights, heights, heights be - come
heights, heights, heights, heights, heights be - come

63
mp
poco rit.
D
Simply ♩ = c.56
To ev-'rything a sea-son.
fear - some, (mm)
fear - some, (mm)
fear - some, (mm)
fear - some, (mm)
p
mf warm
con molto Ped.
SOPRANO SOLO
S. Solo
68
mf espress.
When sud-den bird-song is a - larm-ing, a - larm - ing,
f ma dolce
71
mf
f
and sweet daugh-ters sing, sing out of

74
mf
mp dolce
tune,
When
e-ven ho-ney bees
are
mf
mp
LH
77
mf
p
mp
mf float
irk-some
though the
ap-ple is in blos-som,
is in
blos - som,
ah
mf
mp dolce
80
f
When sud-den bird - song, bird - song
is a -
f
83
mf
-larm - ing
and
sweet daugh-ters sing, sing
out of tune,
sing out of
mf

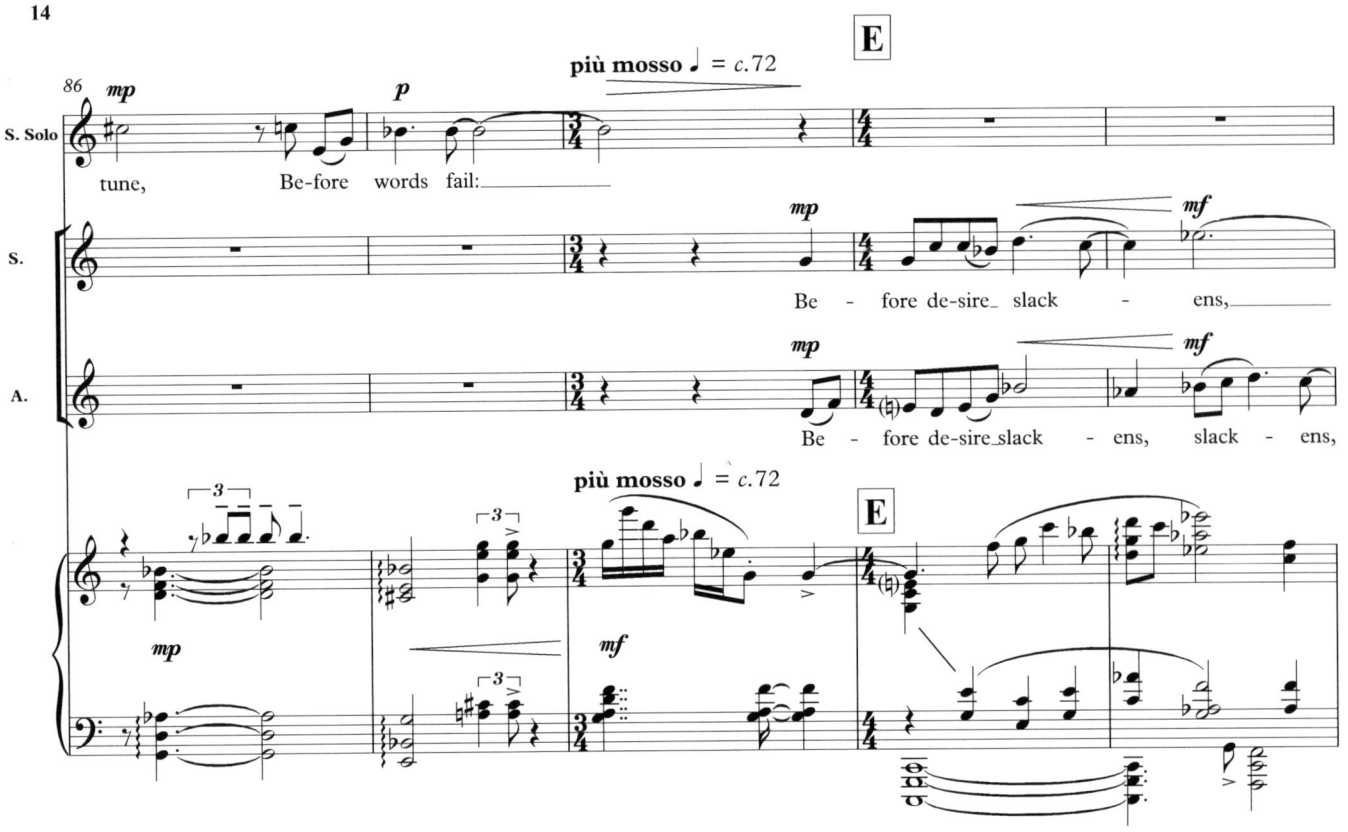
86
mp
p
più mosso ♩ = c.72
E
S. Solo
tune, Be-fore words fail:
S.
mp
mf
Be - fore de-sire slack - ens,
A.
mp
mf
Be - fore de-sire slack - ens, slack - ens,
più mosso ♩ = c.72
E
mp
mf

91
UPPER VOICES
mp
U.V.
To ev - 'ry thing a sea - son,
S.
mf
f
Be - fore the al-pha-bet scram - bles, de - sire
A.
mf
f
Be - fore the al-pha-bet scram - bles, de - sire
T.
mf
f
de-sire slack-ens, a sea-son,
B.
mf
mf
f
de-sire slack-ens, To ev - 'ry thing a sea-son, a sea-son,

95
Sus. Cym. (soft sticks)
To ev - 'ry thing a sea - son.
slack-ens, be - fore words fail, words
slack-ens, be - fore words fail, words
de - sire slack-ens, be - fore words fail, words
de - sire slack-ens, be-fore words fail, words
To Tambourine
100
Cym.
S.
A.
T.
B.
fail, words fail:
fail, words, words fail:
fail, words, words fail:
fail, words, words fail:
F Cheerful, steady but with bounce ♩ = c.96
Tambourine
mf leggiero
(con Ped.)

107
Tamb.
mf
UPPER VOICES
mf leggiero
U.V.
a time to plant, and a time to pluck up that which is
8vb
113
mp
plant - ed;
A time to kill, and a time to heal, a time to
119
mf
mf
heal;
A time to kill and a time to heal; a
125
mp
time to break down,
and a time to build, to

131
U.V.
build, build up;
S.
mf
build, build up;
A.
mf
build, build up;
137
mp espress.
A time to weep,
mp
ah
mp
ah
LH
RH
mp espress.
143
mf
and a time to laugh;
mf
ah
mf
ah
mf

149
mf
a time to mourn, and a
ah
ah
155
time to dance, to dance, a
mf
dance, dance,
mf
dance, dance,
161
time to mourn, and a time to dance, to dance;
mf
dance,
mf
dance,

167
to dance;
to dance;
f
173
G
Tamb.
Tamb.
mf
UPPER VOICES 1
U.V. 1
mf
A time to cast a-way stones, and a time to ga-ther stones to-
UPPER VOICES 2
U.V. 2
mf
A time to cast a-way
G
mf
179
mp
-ge - ther, ga-ther stones to - ge - ther, ga - ther stones to-
mp
stones, and a time to ga-ther stones to - ge - ther, ga-ther stones to - ge - ther;

185
-ge-ther; a time to em-brace, and a time to re-frain, re - frain from em - brac - ing;
mp
a time to em-brace, and a time to re-frain, re - frain from em -
191
-brac - ing;
f
197
mp
a time to keep, and a time to cast a -
mp
A time to get, and a time to lose; a time to keep, and a time to cast a -
mf

202
Tamb.
U.V. 1
-way;
U.V. 2
-way;
S.
f
cast a - way;
A.
f
cast a - way;
f
208
H
To Sus. Cym.
mf
mf
A time to rend, and a time to sew; a time to keep
mf
A time to rend, a time to rend, and a time to sew; a time to keep
H
mf

214
mp
mf
si - lence, and a time to speak;
mp
mf
si - lence, and a time to speak;
mp
f
ah
ah
mp
f
ah
ah
mp
mf
220
f
f
A
f
f
A
ah
ah
f
A
f
A
f

226
UPPER VOICES 1 & 2
U.V.
time to love, and a time to hate, to love;
S.
f
love,
A.
f
love,
T.
time to love, and a time to hate, to love;
B.
time to love, and a time to hate, to love;
232
f
a time of war, and a time of peace, of
love;
love;
f
a time of war, and a time of peace, of
f
a time of war, and a time of peace, of

238
I Simply ♩ = c.66
peace.
f
ah
ah
f
ah
ah
peace.
ah
peace.
ah
I Simply ♩ = c.66
mf
(con Ped.)
244
SOPRANO SOLO
S. Solo
J
mf espress.
3
The wind drives south,
S.
mp
The wind
A.
mp
The wind
T.
mp
The wind
B.
J
f espress.
3
mf
LH

249
mf
the wind wafts, north, north wind
drives south,
drives south,
drives south,
The wind drives south,
254
wafts north.
mf
the wind wafts north, wafts north.
mf
the wind wafts north, wafts, wafts north.
mf
the wind wafts north, wafts, wafts north.
mf
the wind wafts north.
LH

258
K
U.V.
S.
dan - ces in,
A.
dan - ces in,
T.
One ge - ne - ra - tion stum - bles, the next skips and dan - ces in,
B.
One ge - ne - ra - tion stum - bles, the next skips and dan - ces in,
K
262
SOPRANO SOLO
S. Solo
dan - ces in,
UPPER VOICES
U.V.
There is no - thing new, there is no - thing new un - der the sun,
S.
dan - ces in,
sun,
A.
dan - ces in,
dan - ces in, in,
T.
dan - ces in, no - thing, no - thing,
B.
dan - ces in, no - thing, no - thing,
mf dolce

267
Sus. Cym.
mf
dan - - ces in.
mf
there is no-thing new un-der the sun,
sun,
mf
dan - ces
dan - ces in,
mf
dan - ces
no - thing, no - thing, dan - ces in,
mf
no - thing, no - thing, dan - ces in,
mf dolce

272
Cym.
U.V.
there is no-thing new un-der the sun,
S.
in, sun,
A.
in, sun, un-der the, un-der the sun,
T.
dan - ces in, un-der the sun,
B.
dan - ces in, un-der the sun,
L
276
S.
Be - fore dead-ly clouds, clouds mass and close ranks, un-der the sun,
A.
Be - fore dead-ly clouds, clouds mass and close ranks,
T.
Be-fore, be-fore clouds mass, close ranks,
B.
Be-fore, be-fore dead-ly clouds mass, there is no-thing new un-der the
L

280
SOPRANO SOLO
M
S. Solo
fall, fall,
S.
Be - fore grids seize and tur - bines fall, fall, fall, fall,
A.
Be - fore grids seize and tur-bines fall, fall, fall, fall,
T.
un-der the sun, Be - fore grids seize and tur-bines fall, fall,
B.
sun, Be - fore grids seize and tur-bines fall, fall,
M
dolce
285
mf dim. poco a poco
fall fall si - - - - lent,
fall, fall, fall, fall, fall, fall si - lent, si - lent,
fall, fall, fall, fall, fall si - lent, si - lent,
fall, fall, fall si - lent, si - lent,
fall, fall, fall si - - lent,
LH
mf dim. poco a poco

290
S. Solo
U.V.
there is no-thing new un-der the sun,
S.
ah
A.
T.
B.
be-fore the sea cur - dles, ah
mp dolce
295
there is no-thing new, no-thing,
Be - fore plates grind and wi - den, and this
Be - fore plates grind, grind and wi - den,
LH

299
f
no-thing, no-thing, there is no-thing new,
poor, poor pla - net spins,
poor pla - net spins, spins,
poor pla - net spins, spins,
pla - - net spins,
LH
302
N
mf cresc.
S.
Be - fore the hub
A.
Be - fore the hub
T.
Be-fore the hub
B.
spins,
Be-fore the hub
N
f

306
SOPRANO SOLO
S. Solo
ah
U.V.
there is no-thing new, no-thing,
S.
black-ens and ex-plodes,
A.
black-ens and ex-plodes,
T.
black-ens and ex-plodes,
B.
black-ens and ex-plodes,
310
poco rit.
meno mosso ♩ = 56
mf espress.
mf quasi recit.
a tempo
be-fore the moon wastes and con-stel-la-tions are snuffed out.
mp warm

O
l'istesso tempo ♩ = 56
314
S.
A.
T.
B.
p
mf
mp
*Be - fore dust falls to dust, be -
ah
*Be - fore dust falls to dust, be -
p resonant
LH
RH
Sus. Cym.
319
-fore dust falls to dust and the spi - rit soars,
-fore dust falls to dust
-fore dust falls to dust soars,
-fore dust falls to dust spi - rit soars,
f
*Dies irae sequence

323
To Triangle
Cym.
U.V.
there is no-thing new un-der the sun,
S.
the spi-rit soars, spi - rit soars, be-
A.
the spi - rit soars, spi - rit soars, be-
T.
the spi - rit soars, spi - rit soars, be-
B.
spi - rit soars, be-
bell-like
327
there is no-thing new un-der the sun,
-fore dust falls to dust, dust falls to
-fore dust falls to dust, dust falls to
-fore dust falls to dust, dust falls to
-fore dust falls to dust, dust falls to

331
mp
there is no-thing new un-der the sun,
dust,
dust to
dust,
dust to
dust,
dust to
dust,
dust to
f
335
SOPRANO SOLO
mf espress.
with a hand-ful of quiet - ness
mp cresc.
draw near
S. Solo
S.
A.
T.
B.
mf
dust,
dust to dust,
LH
RH

339
S. Solo
to your cre - a - tor.
U.V.
there is no - thing new,
S.
dust, dust,
A.
dust, dust,
T.
dust, dust,
B.
dust, dust,
dim. poco a poco
343 Triangle
Tri.
ritardando
lunga
there is no-thing new, there is no - thing new.
dust, dust.
mp dolce